Out Of The Tunnel

A True Story of One Woman's Life and Experience of Schizophrenia

JOAN WICKS

DEDICATION

To my husband, my five beautiful children, friends and family, for all their care and support through my illness.

To the medical profession, who did the best they could.

To my three "unseen doctors", who showed me the way to overcome obstacles I encountered.

To my dear Lord, who has never left me to tread my path alone and unprotected.

CONTENTS

FOREWORD

My story has been written in the hope that it may create a better understanding of schizophrenia: for other sufferers and their families; for nurses, who have a very limited understanding of the experience of schizophrenia; also to help the general public understand some forms of mental illness.

When you have read this story, you will realize that any form of mental illness can happen to anyone, often when you least expect it. I would like to add that I have never shown any signs of violence or anger in all the thirty years I have had this illness. This is much more usual than the media acknowledges.

1 CHILDOOD

BIRTH

A tiny being emerges into the light
"Here we are again," it says sighing.
Another journey begins and all the hardships
That have been endured, come with me.

The Family of Man is now my family
And I must play my part.
Even now, even at this early stage
I choose the path of longing.

Dreams will have their effect on
This tiny child and hope will light its way.
All alone and vulnerable, untouched
And untouchable, it finds its Star.

And all its life this Star will beckon.
Unbeknown to other men, it hears
The music that only this Star can produce.
One day it will call "Come Home."

Joan.

Dear reader, you may be wondering why I have gone back to the beginning of my life to write my story, even though I didn't suffer from Schizophrenia till I was 43 years old. I feel it is important to include my childhood, as we are affected by it all our lives and it colours the way we live, almost unconsciously. So, travel with me through my life, and you may understand the signposts to the illness that has had such an effect on me.

I was born on the 5th August 1941, in a little town in Wiltshire. Six weeks premature and weighing only 4lb I was placed in an incubator. My dad was in the R.A.F. stationed in lots of places and later parachuted into Germany. He never talked about his experiences during the war, but I think he went through a lot. I spent the next two years travelling with Mum, to places where my dad was stationed, until my sister Rachael was born in Chelmsford.

After the war was over we went to Lancaster and lived with my mum's friend Lizzie, where my sister Tricia was born. My dad sat in the council offices for two weeks trying to get us a council house. He eventually succeeded and we moved to a council estate in Lancaster. It was a three-bedroomed house with a large garden. My happiest memories of these early days were laughing and playing with my two sisters.

FOUR YEARS OLD.

Dance lightly Joan, in this dawn of your life.
A thousand beasts wait patiently to devour you.
But carefully, you learn to walk and talk
And stand unafraid of the Giant Cat.

On the ceiling in your room, a myriad scenes
Pass across your view. Knights and princesses,
Witches and kingdoms of fairytale lands
That are as real as the warm fire downstairs.

You inhabit many worlds and make
No distinction between them, such as
"This is real, this is unreal."
You are too busy watching the joy unfold.

And into this world comes food and warm clothing,
Blankets, soft pillows, and two sisters to laugh with.
Not for you the sounds of war
That plague your parents in the night.

Joan.

My dad used one of the bedrooms in our new house as a place to mend watches and clocks, which he was very good at. My earliest memories are being afraid of his voice, which was always stern. We had to be silent during meals and were taught to say Grace: "Thank you God, for my good dinner; please can I get down?" I was never sure if it was God I was asking to get down or my dad. If we spoke during meals we were sent into a corner or out in the passage. If I was sent in the passage, I used to play pretend games with pretend people.

My dad would sometimes sing songs to us and it was when he did this that I felt love for him. Mum was lovely and worked hard to look after me and my sisters. I used to lie in bed at night listening to my mum and dad having rows and sometimes I would hear him hitting her and my mum crying. I was very frightened, and would pray to God to stop them fighting.

I started school, in a nearby Church school, about five streets away. Rachael, Tricia, and I used to walk to school, as my parents never came to school. We were also never allowed to bring friends to our house and we were told never to talk about our home life at school, or to our friends.

Rachael and I had misbehaved in some way and my dad punished us by sitting us both on a dining chair back to back and tying us to them with rope. It may have been because Rachael and I had a competition about who could eat the most slices of bread and jam. I ate ten and Rachael ate eight. We didn't realise they could hardly afford the bread.

I woke up one night to hear strange sounds coming from my parent's room and I heard a baby crying. I was so excited, I woke Rachael up and said, "Mum's got something." Rachael said "Is it a new powder puff?" In the morning my dad took Rachael, Tricia, and me to meet our new baby sister, who was going to be called Ruth. I thought she was so lovely and very dainty.

So our life went on. There was not a lot of money but my sisters and I played in the garden, collecting cobwebs off the trees and playing with caterpillars we found, which I used to stroke, until my eyes became red and swollen and then I stopped playing with them.

Rachael, Tricia and I enjoyed going to school. We had an assembly every morning with hymns and prayers. All I can remember is playing with three balls against a wall and skipping, which I loved, and playing with my friends. We had film shows twice a week, which we really enjoyed, except for the time Tricia wet herself. We sat at a desk in school and wrote with nib pens and inkwells. We used to visit a sweet shop on the way to school, when mum gave us a penny each. There was also car dump close to the school with lots of old car wrecks. We used to play in them and pretend we were going on long journeys to faraway lands.

Two of my dad's favourite sayings were "Children should be seen and not heard," and "Little pigs have big ears". My mum and dad had a special language they had invented, so that we wouldn't know what they were talking about. My sisters and I had secret meetings when my parents weren't around. We used to laugh a lot together and these times were very special to me.

My dad kept a lot of chickens in the back garden, which he fattened up till nearly Christmas, then would humanely kill them and sell them to a lot of our neighbours for their Christmas dinner. It was my job to deliver them and collect the money.

Another sister, Jean, arrived, with blonde hair and blue eyes. She was our baby. I think I was seven when I changed my first nappy. When Jean was very small, she found a tin of talcum powder and sprinkled it all over my parent's bedroom. I expect that took some cleaning.

Mum got a job in a fish and chip shop but Dad wasn't very happy about this, so he got a job in the same fish and chip shop, frying fish. Rachael and I were left to look after the three younger sisters. We were both under ten. We were very scared one night when lots of daddy long legs came in the living room. We thought Dad had put them in.

I was always caring about children who didn't have enough to eat. I asked a little boy, on the way to school "What have you eaten today?" He replied "Just peas," so I asked my mum for some food for him.

Our time at that house came to an end and my dad rented a council shop with living accommodation in a little village just a few miles from Lancaster. My dad started the shop with a bag of onions, which gradually became fruit and vegetables, then fresh fish which he used to get from Morecambe. The fish were so fresh, we used to watch them jumping in the sink full of water in the shop. Being the eldest I served in the shop, but I have the feeling my dad only asked me to do that with customers he didn't like. I was ten years old. My dad bought a van and built up a round out in the country. I used to go with him to help and would be given a treat of fresh haddock and bread and butter when we arrived home.

We also used to deliver papers in the evening, to all the houses on our estate. My dad collected the papers from a house in the village. Every Tuesday, we went to the village Hut and paid sixpence to watch "Flash Gordon" films. We loved them. Mum and Dad had more money, so there was lots to eat and sometimes my dad would take us to the beach at Morecambe, to play on the sand and paddle in the sea. We did have some happy times. I spent a lot of my time looking after my sisters, whom I loved dearly, but they have told me that sometimes I used to smack them (not hard) so I could hug them better. Well, it must be true.

I travelled by bus every day to a secondary modern school in Lancaster for a year. I didn't like the school very much as it was very strict and dark with Victorian classrooms. It was also much larger than my primary school and I was overwhelmed by so many children. I cannot remember having any friends there, so it was all a blur. I did what was asked of me, but I really only lived in my own dream world.

I was very happy when my dad decided to sell the shop and move to Devon.

2 WE ALL MOVE TO DEVON.

After my dad decided we were all leaving the shop and moving to Devon, he bought a large removal van. He loaded it with all our possessions and set off with Rachael, Tricia and me sitting on the front seat with him. Mum went on the train with Ruth and Jean. It was a very exciting journey, as there were no motorways then and each town we went through seemed like a new and magical place. The Devonshire countryside was so soft and gentle, not a bit like the rugged North. It had red soil!

We were going to stay at my grandma's guest house in Torquay. I loved my grandma very much as Rachael and I had spent many happy holidays with her when we were little in Blackpool, where she and my grandad ran a boarding house before they moved to Torquay.

The guest house in Torquay was one of our favourite places, as sometimes we spent family Christmases there. It had twelve bedrooms, a large dining room, lounge and conservatory and family living accommodation with a large kitchen. There was a long banister which my sisters and I used to slide down every morning. To entertain all the adults at Christmas we sang songs, danced and recited poems. My grandma lived with her son, my uncle John, who waited on tables and played the piano. He was my mum's brother. His wife, my Aunt Ismay, did the cooking with my grandma for the visitors in the summer season. I loved my aunt very much, as she had taught me my first prayer when I was seven. "Gentle Jesus, meek and mild, look upon a little child, pity my simplicity, suffer me to come to thee."

We all stayed with them while my dad looked around the area for a shop. He finally found a corner shop with living accommodation in Dawlish. I remember feeling sad at leaving my grandma, uncle and aunt. They were always so loving towards me and my sisters.

The shop was a general store and sold fruit and vegetables, groceries, biscuits and sweets. Unlike today, the biscuits were loose in glass-topped containers and sold in paper bags by weight, as also were the sweets in large jars. My dad sliced ham and bacon on the slicing machine and cut cheese from large round cheeses.

When we had all settled in, the younger girls attended a nearby primary school and I went to a secondary modern school half a mile away, which I walked to every day. It was a lovely school and I was very happy there and worked hard at my lessons until in the final year I became Head Girl which was a great surprise to me.

I served in the shop every day after school, when I wasn't looking after my sisters or helping Mum. It hurts me to write about this but one day I came home to find a family upset concerning my sister Rachael. My dad was angry with her, so I stood up for her and tried to reason with him. He hit me very hard and proceeded to hit me up the stairs, when he knocked me into the bath. I cried so much.

Most of my life during my childhood, I was very afraid of my dad. When he was angry his nostrils flared and his eyes were cold and hard. He had been a boxer, before the war, so I felt it whenever he hit me. I think I was afraid of my dad until the day I was married, when he actually cried at my wedding. I know that he suffered a lot from the experiences he had in the war. He never spoke of it, but mum told me he used to wake up screaming after he came home. He suffered from terrible migraines and I often prayed for him to get better.

For a long time, I buried my feelings about the way he treated me and always told myself I loved my mum and dad. I prayed to God a lot; after all, He was someone who would not hurt me and Jesus taught us to love one another, so of course, I must love my dad.

At the weekends I would take my sisters on long walks or to the playing fields, but on Sunday we all went to Sunday school. Later, as we got older, we attended church; either the Congregational Church or the Methodist Church.

About that time, my youngest sister, Vicki, was born. We all sat on the stairs waiting for Mum to give birth. We all thought she was just beautiful. Dad said he could tell it was another girl by her cry. There was a lot for me to do with a new baby in the house, as Mum needed a great deal of help.

We weren't always well behaved girls. I remember one Sunday morning, Rachael, Tricia and I were all sleeping in a double bed. We made up a game of pushing each other out of bed with our feet, by leaning against the window. It was my turn to lean against the window, which I did, then the whole window fell out onto the pavement below, just missing an old lady on her way to church. The Salvation Army was playing music outside. Dad was furious, so we kept out of his way. It didn't help matters when the pane of glass he bought to replace the old one split in half on the bed.

A few doors away from the shop there was a cobbler's shop and I was friendly with the disabled man who owned it. I would call in and chat to him on the way home from school, to watch him mending shoes, cutting the leather and stitching the soles. The shop had a wonderful smell of leather which I can still remember.

I recall, another time, when Rachael and I were in bed. She was much more daring than I was. She decided to tear her nightdress to make it into a dressing gown. We laughed so much at the noise of each tear, then Mum came in and told Rachael she must sit on their bed and sew it before Dad came home. Of course she managed, with big stitches, to finish it before his return.

My dad had a stall in Newton Abbot Market, which was held every Saturday. Sometimes I went with him to serve. We sold curly pats of butter, cheese and fresh eggs. It was fun talking to the other stallholders and having cups of tea and buns.

During the summer holidays, we all used to meet up in two cars, with my grandma, uncle and aunt and their little daughter Elaine, who was the same age as Vicki, and they loved playing together. We would spend a happy day in the country, having lovely fry-ups on a primus stove and making cups of tea, usually with home-made cake. I used to love gazing out of the car window at the stars and street lights on the drive home.

My Dad gave us pocket money of two pence for every year of our age and I used to save mine and buy make-up secretly as I wasn't allowed to wear it at fourteen. I had a place at Torquay Technical College to study Domestic Science and travelled each day by train with three friends. I would put some make-up on in the train and wipe it off on the way home. I enjoyed college and used to have lunch at my grandma's, as their hotel was quite near. As well as learning household cleaning, I also did lots of cooking and would take home delicious meals for the family. It was a two year course but I only completed one year, as Mum and Dad were very short of money and I needed to get a job to help them financially.

I passed an interview for a job in a chemist in Teignmouth and was given a post in the drug department. It was very interesting, with a few new experiences. I remember an elderly lady came in who had hurt her ankle. I gave her a cream to rub in and some painkillers to take. She came back a week later and I asked her how her ankle was healing. She said the cream was fine but she didn't know how taking tablets by mouth could possibly help her ankle. So she had crushed the tablets in water, dipped a bandage in the water, wrapped it round her ankle and it worked fine. I smiled to myself but who knows? It may have worked better than swallowing them.

One day at work, a woman asked me for a tube of Volpar paste. I thought it was a rheumatic cream but I couldn't find it anywhere. I called to Robin, the young dispenser, "Where do we keep the Volpar paste?" He told me to send her to the surgical department, then come and see him. He said it was a contraceptive paste and then proceeded to give me my first sex education and told me to go to the surgical department and memorise the other items we kept for that purpose. I was very embarrassed but I learnt a lot that day.

I began to smoke cigarettes in the staff room, as everybody smoked. I hated it first of all but I persevered because I wanted to be grown up. In those days it was considered the accepted thing to do and cigarettes were only sixpence a packet! I remember smoking a cigarette in one of the stock rooms when the manager of the shop came in. I hastily put the cigarette in my pocket. He said, "Joan, I think you are on fire!" Smoke was pouring out of my pocket.

I earned £4.10 per week; I gave £4 to mum and had 10 shillings for myself. I travelled by bus from Dawlish to Teignmouth and usually wore a circular skirt with lots of petticoats, V neck sweater, three quarter length white gloves and after I had mastered smoking, a black cigarette holder.

I wanted to act, so I got a part in the yearly pantomime, singing and dancing in the chorus. After this I joined the Amateur Dramatic Society and was given a part as a talking shop dummy in a play called "Man Alive". I loved dancing and each week in Dawlish an Old Time Dance was held in a building known as The Hut. I wore a white low-necked blouse and a black taffeta skirt and would dance lots of different Old Time dances, my favourite being the Veleta. Later I learnt to Jive when Rock and Roll came in, also to do the Twist.

The shop began to lose money, mostly because of customers not paying their bills. So mum and dad sold the shop, and we moved to a house by the stream in Dawlish. It was a happy time in lots of ways and I loved my sisters dearly. We had lots of fun together, especially when the fairground came to town.

I had a bike accident. It was a man's bicycle and I tried to put my right leg across the crossbar but my left leg twisted at the knee and I fell, with the bike on top of me. As a result my whole left leg was in plaster for three months. I remember hobbling up to the pulpit in Church to sing a hymn. "There was ninety and nine that safely lay, in the shelter of the fold. But one was out on the hills away, far off from the Gates of Gold." A young man came up to me afterwards and said "You sang like an angel. That was beautiful." Nobody ever said anything like that to me.

My dad became a dedicated stamp collector, which he remained till his death. He worked as a toolmaker for a firm in Exeter, and as the house was quite large, my mum took in a few people for bed and breakfast.

One day, I was nursing my sister Vicki, who was 18 months old, when she slipped off my knee onto the floor. My dad was so angry with me that he hit me hard across the face, hit me up the stairs then knocked me down them. These outbursts of his happened quite often, once because I had taken a flannel off a younger sister. I don't think many of my sisters were hit by my dad, except perhaps Rachael, so he may have mellowed with the passing years. It must have been hard for Mum and Dad, bringing up six girls and always a shortage of money.

One day, I was looking out of the window, which overlooked the stream, with my sister Tricia, when I saw a young man opposite who was standing by the Fire Station. I said to her, "That's my professor."

It was the first time I saw Peter, the love of my life.

3 MY FIVE LOVELY SISTERS

RACHAEL

I lit your candle this morning
While the snow was falling
And thought of you, so far away
In another land, living your life.

We have shared so many times
Of Pooh and Piglet and Treacle Mines
And while I burned with Love's intensity
You danced gaily in the flames.

Not for us the crochet or the knitting.
We have built an altar to Love,
Where pain and suffering are healed
And age and dying hold no fears.

Pavarotti is singing and I am dancing.
Your shadow dances with me
And just for a moment, we are together.
There is no such place as far away

Joan.

You have already met my sister Rachael, but I would like to say a little about how she has enriched my life. She lives in Cyprus now with her husband and I talk to her on the phone, two or three times a week. When she lived in Devon at a hotel that she and her husband had bought, I used to visit her for a holiday sometimes with some of my children. They had three boys and the children would play together. Rachael and I had wonderful evenings, playing music, drinking brandy, smoking and sharing our experiences of life.

Compared with me she is much quieter and gentler. I cook food enough to feed an army, while she creates small meals with exciting ingredients. She cuts a cake four times and just eats a small piece. She has lots of little dishes with small amounts of leftovers in her fridge.

She is a wonderful painter and some of her work has been displayed in exhibitions in Cyprus. A few years ago she had a Near Death Experience, during an operation and it has changed her vision of Life ever since.

We are both elderly ladies now and we have lots of laughs about the changes that happen due to age.

She has visited a few times with her husband and by herself.

I feel so blessed to have her as my sister.

TRICIA

You are one of my beautiful sisters
And have a heart of gold.
Not aware of how special you are
Shining with an inner light
That spreads as you grow old.

I marvel at your awareness,
The way you always have an answer
To our questions. Where does it come from?
A place inside of you, that is clear and bright,
Helping us all to see the light

I feel privileged to know you,
Sharing some special times.
Your home is a place of refuge for all.
In happy times and sad
You give us hope and make us glad.

You have had your share of pain and sorrow
Worked hard all of your life
Yet you have time for everyone.
You have filled my life with happiness
And healed the pain with love,
With laughter, and with Joy

Joan.

Tricia is a very special part of my life, I phone her every other day and she has helped me so much, especially when I was ill. She always knows how to tell me to slow down and relax, as I always get excited when I have a new project or dream to pursue.

Many years ago she came to stay with me and Peter. He invited a very close friend of his, called Dave to come and take my sister out. They fell in love with each other and a few years later were married. They had three lovely children, two girls and one boy.

They came to visit us for holidays over the years and we spent many happy hours together, drinking home-made nettle beer and playing cards. Sadly dear Dave died suddenly, just after he retired. It was a blow to all the family and Tricia was heartbroken.

It has been twelve years and she has been so strong and brave. She has five wonderful grandchildren now, and her home is lovely. I have spent some great holidays with her over the past few years, when I have been well, and hope to one day go again, even though Plymouth is a long way from Lancashire and we are both older.

She is my very dear sister.

RUTH

Not yesterday, or today, or tomorrow
But a long time ahead,
Our true meeting waits for us
In another land.

We have so many shared memories
No need to remind you
We carry out the sacred task
As best we are able
And thank God for it.

If we had not been sisters, we would have been friends
Both drawn, by the longing and the silences
You have spoken in your art, and in your writing
And I have wept at your perception.

Sometimes our truth falls on the Desert
And greed waits at the door.
We talk for a while, strengthening the bond.
Thank God you are always there

Love binds our hearts together
And laughter dances with us.
Keep heart, dear sister,
And forever watch the Stars

Joan.

Ruth lives in a flat in Bath, with her husband. She is very creative and spends a lot of her time painting beautiful pictures, writing a book and making wonderful costumes for the plays her son produces in London. He is doing "Macbeth" at present. He is a talented actor as well and gives her a lot of joy. She also has a lovely daughter living near London, also a son who lives in Cornwall. I have spent great times with her and once, for a while, we lived in the same village in Somerset and spent a lot of our days together.

We are both interested in following Sufi Teaching; we study a lot of books on Sufism. She is the only sister I can share this part of my life with. I love her very much and have always felt protective toward her, since she was a little girl.

She has been through some difficult experiences in her life, due to illness and family relationships. At times they have hurt her a lot but she is very courageous and does a lot of work on healing herself.

It makes me very happy to have her as my sister.

JEAN

A beautiful woman walks along the shore
Barefoot, in Grecian robes, with flowers in her hair.
She dreams her private dreams
And shares, only with her Lord, her secret longings.

By her side walks a golden haired child.
Laughing at the freedom she feels at last.
It is my sister, Jean, in her many disguises,
hiding her secret self from prying eyes.

I will not pry into your special world, dear Sister.
Your gentle humour, and caring spirit,
Touch everyone you meet.
We, your sisters, embrace you.

You suffer your trials in silence
And the joy, from which you were separated
So young, waits patiently to be renewed.
Hold my hand, dear Sister and together
We will wait for the tide.......

Joan.

Jean is the House Manager of a block of Independent Retirement flats in Shropshire and has living accommodation in the same building with her husband, who is also a relief manager for the same organisation. He sadly had a heart attack a few years ago but is now completely recovered. They have two lovely girls and four grandchildren. She used to make beautiful birthday and Christmas cards in cross stitch. They were very special.

She and her husband are dedicated Christians and this is the most important thing in her life. I can totally understand this; many of us have spiritual Truths that are the essence of our lives. I know she feels that she suffers from lack of self-esteem, but with the love and humour she gives to everyone, it's hard to believe she has this problem. I think we all of us, my sisters and I, have this, probably as the effect of our childhood, and being denied the chance to step out into the world.

She has suffered with illness these past few years. She has had cancer of the thyroid, arthritis and lately trouble with her eyes; very bad cataracts. She has had depression and family traumas but her faith in Christ's love and healing has been the most important thing to guide her through it all.

Although she is a very private person, I am happy to know her and love her as my sister.

VICKI

I knew you for such a little while
When you were young and I your elder sister.
Such a happy child, so full of laughter
Only a few years old, when I left home.

I never knew the path you trod
Or how life treated you
But you're lovely singing voice
Echoed around the dark times of my life.

Remember fondly the rare occasions;
We have shared little life.
Sometimes happy, sometimes sad
Marvelled at your exuberance.

I do not know what the road ahead
Holds, for any one of us,
But if I could, I would have you tread
A road perfumed with flowers
And filled with song.

You have recently lost Warren,
A husband you loved so much.
We all grieve with you, at your loss,
As you try and face this bitter blow.

Joan

My sister Vicki is a very special person. Although she has coped with depression, she has a wonderful love of life and I feel happy to know her. She has a beautiful singing voice and has performed in many places in the West Country. I have tapes of her singing, which I often play to cheer me when I feel low. She is also a writer, who has had stories published. She is great at saying "I can do this and I will." This she has learnt through her reading and experience of life.

She has had 37 years of married life with Warren, and she has been very happy, until she needed her strength and courage to nurse him through the cancer which cost him his life.

She has nine lovely grandchildren and a son Peter, and Warren's two daughters, Dawn and Jenny. We all feel what she is going through at this time, and will help her all we can.

God bless you Darling. You are my lovely sister.

4 A LOVE MATCH

Peter

There is a man who shares my life.
If you met him, he would make you smile.
In my heart he has a very special place:
Husband, lover, soul mate and friend.

We have walked the Path of Life together
For many years and he has been my rock,
Father of five beautiful children
And lover of the beauty in life.

Music, animals and birds, sweet scented
Flowers and trees, speak to his heart.
And his love for God, although he will deny it,
Is every day apparent.

It has not always been an easy road.
There have been trials along the way.
We have both known pain and loss
And Love has been a healing balm.

There are not many like him
In this world and I feel blessed.
He's not an angel, just a man
Who thought to care for me.

Joan.

I was walking on the lawn in Dawlish centre, when I saw Peter in front of me. I caught up with him at the level crossing, on the bridge over the stream. He looked at me and said the words I have always remembered,

"Shall we cross together?"

We walked down to the railway bridge beside the sea and he bought some raffle tickets to win a car. Then he asked me if I would like to go for a cup of tea. We went to a nearby café and he bought tea and cakes. He told me many years later that he had kept the crumbs from my plate in a serviette.

That is how our love began. Then he took me home and met my mum, who always liked him. He was about five feet, nine inches tall with black curly hair, green eyes, glasses, and very slim. In fact he was often mistaken for Buddy Holly.

One evening, Peter and I went to see the film, "The Student Prince" with Edmond Purdom and Ann Blyth, a wonderful film, dubbed with the lovely singing voice of Mario Lanza singing the love songs. Mum came with us to chaperone me as I was only fifteen and a half years old. It was such a romantic film, perfect for two people falling in love. Afterwards Mum waited in Dad's car, while Peter and I walked to the beach to look at the sea, stars and a beautiful moon. He kissed me, and for the first time I noticed the wonderful smell he had, which completely intoxicated me; I was falling in love. He held my hand and I thought he had wonderful hands, long fingers; a musician's hands. He told me he played the violin.

We went out together for a few weeks. Peter would call at our house, to see if I was allowed out. At times, Dad would say I wasn't allowed out and instead would take Peter to the British Legion Club to play darts. Peter went and amazingly beat him. My parents kept telling me I was too young to have a relationship with a man nearly ten years older than I. So in the end, one night, I told Peter I couldn't see him again. So we parted and I cried all night.

Six months passed, and my mum had a studio photograph taken of my five sisters and me. "Why don't you send one to Peter," she said. Peter was a Cornishman and lived with his parents in Launceston, when he wasn't working as a relief manager for a well known newsagents and booksellers, based in Plymouth.

I sent the photograph and then we began writing letters for a while. Not love letters, just friendly letters. Then one day, I realised I still loved him, so I wrote a letter telling him how much I loved him. At the same time he wrote a letter to me saying he couldn't go on writing friendly letters because he loved me. Our letters crossed in the post. I was working in the chemist and we arranged to meet after I finished work. Peter was coming on his motorbike. We met and fell into each other's arms. I was so happy and so was he. We walked along Teignmouth sea front and then went to a coffee bar and played the Juke Box.

I felt as if I was walking on air and I knew he was the best thing that had ever happened to me.

Peter was given a job relieving the Dawlish shop, so we had lots of time to be together while he stayed in lodgings. He was a practising Spiritualist at that time, learning to be a healer. Sometimes, when we sat on the lawn, he would talk to me about his beliefs and read to me from Spiritualist books, such as "Through the Mists" and "Teachings from White Eagle". He started me on my spiritual search for Truth, by showing me a different way of looking at spiritual experiences.

He also wrote beautiful love letters to me. He is a man of chivalry and high morals, kind to everyone and rarely loses his temper. Nothing I can say could explain my love for him, which somehow transcends normality and is almost a spiritual experience.

Sometimes, we would take my little sister Vicki for a walk in her pram and pretend she was our baby. Twice Peter proposed to me, once on the chairoplanes at the fairground, and another time while sat on a bench in a country lane outside Dawlish.

I remember he kept a small amount of shocking pink wool from my cardigan in his lapel. We were so in love. Our special song has always been "When I fall in love" by Nat King Cole.

About this time, my parents decided to move to Ilfracombe in North Devon and bought a six bed-roomed house to take in visitors for bed and breakfast and evening meal. I applied for a transfer to the same chemist in a branch in Barnstaple, not far from Ilfracombe. Peter came on his motorbike every weekend from wherever he was working and stayed with us. When I was seventeen we got engaged, as my parents now accepted him.

We would go into the hills around Ilfracombe and we had secret places, where we made love for the first time. He was an incredible and amazing lover. We also spent a lot of time in coffee bars talking about our feelings for each other and making plans for our future life together.

I had a new job as secretary and bookkeeper, in an office of a local draper's store. I remember on my first day I was so happy I forgot to go for lunch and was locked in the store by myself. So my boss bought me an alarm clock which he used to set for lunchtime. I really loved the position.

There were four floors in the building. The top floor was the office and sewing room where curtains and cushions were made. The second floor was lingerie, dresses and hats. The ground floor was haberdashery, handbags, dress material and curtain material. In the basement, upholstery was done.

I ordered lace and satin to make my own wedding dress; it was lovely with a long train at the back. My five sisters and my little cousin, Elaine, were going to be bridesmaids. It was one of the happiest days of my life, to be marrying my darling Peter.

We were married March 22nd, 1959 in a Baptist Church, on the street where my family lived. Afterwards, we had a wonderful ten days on a honeymoon at Fowey in Cornwall.

5 MARRIAGE

After Peter and I came home from our honeymoon, we moved into a top floor flat above a tool shop on the high street in Ilfracombe. Peter was away all week working in various towns in the West Country; I continued with my work at the Drapers. I had a very good relationship with my boss, Mister Ted, and we often had long conversations about his life. I operated the telephone intercom, which was connected to all departments, cashed the tills at closing time, typed letters, and worked on the accounts. I was very happy.

Three months after we were married, I became pregnant but carried on with my job. I remember one time when Pete was home, I was having a bath, when I slipped, banged my head on the side of the bath and fainted. Luckily Pete came in, and managed to get me out of the bath and carry me onto the bed, while I was unconscious. I had a wonderful experience of walking by a beautiful river, on my way to somewhere. All the colours were amazing: flowers, grass, trees and a lovely blue sky. I didn't know where I was going, but I felt very happy. Then I woke to find Pete rubbing me with a towel, "I thought I'd lost you," he said and was very upset.

We were happy there and it meant I could visit Mum, Dad and my sisters. After a few months, Pete was made the manager of a newsagents shop in Launceston, his home town in Cornwall. So I had to leave my job and my family and move to Launceston. We lived with Pete's Mum and Dad until the flat over the shop was decorated and ready to move into. At Christmas, hugely pregnant, I sold Christmas cards in the shop.

Helen, our eldest daughter, was born in a maternity home just outside Launceston. She weighed nine pounds and we thought she was just beautiful. I remember thinking: well I've done everything now, what else is there to do in life? Fourteen months later our second daughter, Suzanne, was born at home. I couldn't hold her for sixteen hours as I had a bad hemorrhage and my veins collapsed. The doctor came, and Pete managed to put up a plasma drip in the bedroom. I had an unusual blood group and the doctor couldn't get the blood I needed. It was a very frightening experience for me and my doctor told me I would not be able to have another baby at home. I was at last able to hold our dear little Suzanne. It took a few weeks for me to recover and my life then was very busy with two little girls to care for.

I didn't enjoy my time in Launceston very much, except for Pete and the girls, as Pete worked long hours and sometimes I would feel lonely and miss my sisters and my mum. However, Pete met Mr Hodge, an elderly man, whom he brought up to the flat for a cup of tea. We called him Hodgie. After that he would call most days and he and I would have tea and biscuits and he would tell me of his life as a teacher in Jersey and his exploits during the War. He became a good friend for many years.

I joined the local Amateur Dramatic Society and was given a part in the play "Spring 1600" by Emlyn Williams. I really enjoyed that. We lived in Launceston for a little, and then Pete left the job and was given a position as a buyer in the pen department of a big store in Plymouth. I lived with Pete and the girls in a ground floor flat opposite a cemetery. I made friends with the woman upstairs, who had a little girl. I liked living in Plymouth, as my sister Tricia lived there with her husband and little girl. We met quite often at each other's flats. I would take Helen and Sue to the library to get children's books, to the shops and sometimes to Plymouth Hoe to see the sea. Hodgie would come on the bus to see us most Sundays. I remember one day, I made some strawberry instant whip for Helen and Sue, but I don't think they liked it, as while I was in the kitchen, they plastered each other's hair with it!

Pete's cousin, David, who lived in Plymouth, would often come for a visit with his friend Phil. We had some good times together. I became pregnant again and my son Steve was born. I remember Pete climbing up the outside wall of the hospital to give me a radio to listen to. A doctor was walking past; he must have wondered what was happening. Steve weighed 10 pounds and never stopped eating. He had rice in his bottle at four days old and jars of dinner and pudding at two weeks old. He was a lovely bouncy baby and the girls loved him.

One day the managing director of a pen company met Pete and offered him a salesman's post, travelling to shops in the West Country. Pete took the job, which he loved, and was given a company car, which meant we could have trips out with the children at the weekend.

HALLATROW

I began looking for houses to rent in the Somerset area, which would be more central for Pete's work. I found a farmhouse for rent at £4.50 per week. We took it, and all moved up to a little village called Hallatrow, where we stayed for eight years. It was a lovely 500 year old farmhouse with four bedrooms, bathroom, lounge and a big kitchen with a Rayburn to cook on. During the time we were there, Pete changed his job to a paperback book company with a much larger territory, which he found very interesting.

It was the heady days of the mid sixties; everywhere was peace and love and lots of flowers. I was a typical hippie, long skirts and hair and no shoes for two years.

Pete often met up with hitchhikers, whom he would bring home to stay for a few nights. We made lots of new friends this way, and would stay up late talking philosophy, religion or reading our poetry to each other. We never took drugs, although we enjoyed a few glasses of sherry but mostly drank coffee. We were all high on Life and had great hopes for the future.

Unfortunately, the drug culture spoilt the new wave of Light that was coming in. I often look back on that time and wonder if we will ever again feel the love and light that seemed to permeate around and leave us full of hope.

I had wonderful times with the children. There was a wood nearby, where we would go to pick bluebells and at other times collect blackberries. There was an orchard attached to the farmhouse, where the children used to play. We had lots of picnics in the fields around the village. At night I would read stories to the children or make up stories of my own. There was always lots of music playing which I enjoyed; sometimes Pete would play his classical guitar that we all loved to listen to.

We had a small terrier called Bob, and Helen used to make jumps out of wood and stones for him to jump over. We also had three cats and, if I wasn't careful, they would bring in mice and put them in the playpen for the youngest child. When the children went to bed I would sit with them, but often I fell asleep; they would get up and sneak downstairs to see their dad.

It was about this time that my second son, Jeremy, was born in Bath. I had a vision of him before I even realised I was pregnant. I saw two hands holding a baby in a yellow babygro on the wall of our bedroom; I knew it was a little boy.

We had a close friend called Dennis, whose daughter was Helen's best friend. He came to look after the children while I was giving birth in hospital. Pete was working away, but he came home in time to visit Jeremy and me. Pete's mum also came to stay. I think Steve was upset at me being away, so he tore open a feather pillow and shook the feathers all over the house for my poor mother-in-law to clear up. He also tried to hit a wasp on the window with a hammer and broke the window. As well, he kept driving his pedal car into my mother-in-law's legs. Poor Mum; she had a hard time. He was a bit of a rascal.

I used to send the rented T.V. back to the shop during the summer months, so we could all do other things together. When the children watched T.V. it was always turned off at six pm.

I would often stay up at night to decorate a room, then have a few hours sleep before getting the children up for school in the next village. We used to all walk up a hill, with the youngest in a pram, for the older ones to attend primary school. I remember Jeremy sat in his pram and cried as I went out to him all dressed up for an event at school. I'd put a hat on which I never usually wore. I took the hat off, and he stopped crying. All the washing was done by hand every day. I also made clothes for the children and curtains for the house. Lots of baking was done in the Rayburn and I made my own bread.

Pete's cousin, David, was living with us for a while. He was an artist, and painted some rather unusual pictures on some of the walls. He also used to amuse the children by putting green or red food colouring in the mashed potato.

Something happened while he was staying with us. A huge telephone bill arrived, which I knew he was partly responsible for, and I was devastated. I knew Pete would be upset by it and I didn't know what to do. Wrongly, I decided I'd have to get a job to earn some extra money. So I left the children with David, packed a suitcase and caught a bus to Bristol. The bus driver said "Are you leaving home, Love?" I got off the bus at the railway station and walked onto the platform. Where did I think I was going? I suddenly realized how stupid I was being. I rang my doctor, who said, "Come straight to the surgery," but by this time I felt afraid to get on the bus home, in case everyone was watching me. So I walked sixteen miles home with my heavy suitcase.

When I arrived home, I lay down on the couch and fell asleep. When I woke up, it was to see my doctor and Pete watching me. I was then taken to a mental hospital a few miles away and the nurses put me in a white gown. I was taken to a room and strapped to the floor, where I was then given electric shock treatment. It was barbaric and horrific; thankfully it is different today and only used on rare occasions.

I stayed there ten days and had three lots of E.C.T. Then the psychiatrist said, "We have decided you are not suitable for this treatment." As I left he said, "Well, we have given you a good rest which is probably all you needed". This was my first introduction to mental hospitals and I was terrified by it. I now realise that I was probably suffering from post-natal depression, which was not recognized then. My son was only six months old at the time.

It took me quite a while to recover from this episode of my life. Thank goodness things are improving now in the treatment of mental illness. I have wondered sometimes whether the effect of the E.C.T. could have caused some damage to my brain; I don't suppose I will ever know.

I returned to my happy life at the farmhouse and put this difficult time in the back of my mind. I never asked anyone else to look after our children, except once, when we had some hippies staying. I asked them to watch Steve while I washed the kitchen floor. Luckily I went to check on him and they had let him go outside. He had gone up the drive and onto the main road with cars going past; he was only four years old. Pete managed to bring him back but I always thought after that, I will never trust anyone again with my children.

Hodgie lost his lodgings in Launceston, so we invited him to come and live with us, which he did. We were the family he never had and the children treated him like a grandfather. He stayed with us for a few years and then went into an old people's home in Frome, not far from us. We used to fetch him for the day on Sundays.

My sister Ruth, her husband and two children, boy and girl, came to live in a cottage just up the lane from our farmhouse. It was wonderful to have my sister so near for a few years. The children all played together and Ruth and I had some special times, meeting in each other's houses, sharing our love of books and following the teachings of a great spiritual Master who lived in England.

I made some wonderful friends in Hallatrow; some of them have remained friends all my life. Jim and Carol used to go on picnic trips with us, including their children and ours. When Dennis's first marriage ended, he stayed with us for a while; he was a floor manager in television. Then he met Val, who was a make-up artist in T.V., and they got married. Much later they had two boys who are now married and now have two grandchildren in Australia. They are very close friends and feel like part of my family.

There is also Carol, a very dear friend of mine whom I met when she was twenty and going out with a mutual friend of ours.

I will always be grateful to all these friends, for the love and care they have given me over the many years we have known each other.

The old lady who owned the farmhouse died and her nephew from London inherited her property. We were given six weeks to leave, then we were offered accommodation in the old Police House in Temple Cloud, which was another village about three miles away.

TEMPLE CLOUD

When we moved to the old Police House in Temple Cloud, it was supposed to be for emergency accommodation, until we were given a council house. It had been condemned as a Police house, as there was no bathroom, just an outside toilet. Also there were stone stairs to the three bedrooms, which were always damp. There was a kitchen and two reception rooms downstairs. It was a huge building, with a courthouse in the middle, where magistrates courts were held every week, and a Police house on either side.

Sue and Steve went to a primary school two miles away. We used to walk there every day along a country lane with Jeremy in a pushchair. Helen caught the bus each day to Chew Valley Comprehensive, a few miles away. Later, as Sue got older, she went with Helen.

We did have some good times there, for three years, in spite of the problems with the house that we had to cope with. There were also visits from family and friends, with many happy occasions together. I remember one day, when I found living in that house very difficult, I decided to have a bonfire to cheer myself up. We had a patch of ground just across the driveway that was perfect for a fire. I carried out an armchair and set fire to it, then another armchair; it was quite a blaze. The fire raged until by the end of the afternoon, all that was left in the front room was a standard lamp! I'm amazed the Fire Brigade didn't come. Pete and the children were quite surprised when they got home but I already knew a friend who had a three piece suite and sideboard that she had offered to let me have if I wanted it. Well, it cured my depression and made the family laugh.

When the children had gone to bed and Pete was home, I often went across the road to our local pub for a glass or two of sherry; it was my treat. Pete played his guitar and had a drink while I was away.

When I discovered I was pregnant with our fifth child, I went to see my doctor, who offered me a termination, as I had suffered problems with the previous births. I asked him for a couple of days to make my decision and told him that whatever I decided, I wanted to be sterilized. I went for a walk in the country and stopped by a five barred gate looking over a lovely meadow. I talked to God: "Please help me decide what to do". I looked across the field and had a vision of a beautiful blonde haired little girl with blue eyes, and then I knew I wanted this little girl. We called her Lucy and she has been a joy in our lives. Lucy was born in Paulton Hospital and weighed eight pounds. At first Pete and I didn't know what to call her. I kept thinking Lucy, but we had a guinea pig called Lucy so it didn't seem appropriate. Then Pete came to visit us one day and said, "What about Lucy?" So then I knew it was the right name for her.

Four days later I was sterilized and nearly died under the anaesthetic. It was after this I was told I was allergic to anaesthetics.

I was very busy trying to get us a council house. I had letters from my doctor and wrote to our M.P. Finally, three rats arrived in our dustbin, so I phoned the local councillor and said that we had rats. I told him I would park myself on the council office lawn until we got a house. I had a friend who worked in television, and I said he would come and take pictures.

After three days we were offered a house in Midsomer Norton, so I was grateful to the rats and also to our dear friend, Dennis.

MIDSOMER NORTON

The house we were given to rent by the council had three bedrooms, kitchen, toilet, bathroom and a large lounge. There was a lawn in the garden at the front of the house and at the back of the house was a very long vegetable garden, shed and parking space. At the bottom of the back garden was a lovely oak tree which the children loved to climb. I made oak leaf wine when the leaves turned brown; it tasted just like sherry! We grew masses of vegetables. The yellow courgettes were amazing. I made wine from pea pods and beetroot.

There was a primary school in the field at the bottom of the garden, and Jeremy and Lucy went there. They were very happy at school and did well. Jeremy got the part of Rumpelstiltskin in the Christmas play and was very good. It was a lovely school and I was very involved with what went on and so was Pete. I was a member of the parent teacher association and worked hard at all the events we held.

Helen, Sue and Steve went to a comprehensive school in the town. When Helen left school, she travelled to a polytechnic in Oxford staying in halls of residence. We missed her, but she loved it there and worked hard for her degree. When Sue left school, she went to work in a big store in Bath selling and displaying jewellery. She enjoyed her job and did all the ordering as well.

We all did a lot of cycling in the surrounding countryside. I had a seat on the back of my bike for Lucy. We used to stop sometimes for picnics. It was great fun. We all went swimming at the weekend, then we would come home to listen to the Narnia stories by C.S. Lewis on the radio. We had great trips out in the car on Sunday, visiting National Trust properties, holy sites in Glastonbury, Cheddar Gorge and other well known places.

We had wonderful Christmases there. Pete and I would stay up all night, filling the children's pillow cases and keeping the coal and log fire burning. Pete used to go outside and ring a bell, so the little ones would think it was Father Christmas. It was quite a magical moment to see their faces on Christmas morning.

We had a wonderful holiday for two weeks in a cottage in the Lake District. It was the only holiday we were ever able to afford. Pete and Steve climbed one of the large hills near Keswick. Jeremy found a sheep's skull which he carried on a stick. Lucy got soaking wet running into the sea. We picked rosehips and we and we were a bit afraid of a large bull in a field. The owners of the cottage had left us lots of board games and books to spend our evenings with. We went on a boat across Lake Windermere and walked round some of the lakes. I never realized that one day we would live not very far from this lovely area.

My love for cooking expanded into various experiments with food. A Hunza diet, which involved making chapatti's filled with vegetables and salad from the garden; I tried Chinese cooking, Italian and Indian cooking as well. There were home- made Pizzas and soup and always fried yellow courgettes!

I joined the amateur dramatic society and was given the part of Mama in "I Remember Mama". Sue played the role of my daughter in the play; it was a lot of fun. I did some producing as well, then formed my own Youth Theatre Group which met once a week in two classrooms of the local comprehensive school. I loved it, as I had got tired of the bickering among the adults. There were about forty children and we used to have lots of fun, making up plays and acting them in front of each other. Pete was a Cornishman and always told the children, "Never forget, you are Princes and Princesses of Cornwall," bless him. He loved his children so much and yet he had to be away working and travelling to support us all. He was always so kind, gentle and very funny, but we especially loved hearing him play his guitar. He took some amazing photographs and lovely slides of the family, countryside and birds. He even painted unusual pictures for a while.

I got a job as a care assistant in an old people's home, just a few minutes away. There were just two of us for forty residents and we worked from nine pm till eight am in the morning. The work was hard, but I loved the elderly residents and enjoyed taking care of them. I went home in the morning, got the children ready for school, and then slept till two pm.

It was about this time that our dear friend Hodgie died. We all went to his funeral in Bath, wearing bright coloured clothes, because that was what he wanted. I filled the house with flowers and we played the Kings College Choir, which was the music he loved most.

Sue had met and fallen in love with a nice young man called Henry, and they eventually were married in Bath. Later our first granddaughter, Jade, was born she was lovely.

Pete was now travelling with Magnet selling children's classic books. Then he was made redundant and the company was taken over by

Thomson Publishers. Pete was out of work for about six months, until he was offered a position by Thomson, selling academic books to university bookshops and polytechnics in central England including Wales and the North Country. We then had to make a decision whether to move to the North. After a family discussion, we all wrote tickets with yes and no on, and put them in a hat.

The result was that we all decided to go on the adventure to the North. An aunt lent us £3,000 to put a deposit on a house, and we paid her back over the next few years.

BARNOLDSWICK

After much searching, we travelled to Barnoldswick. On the way we passed Pendle Hill, where the witches once lived and when I saw it, I knew I had come home.

We found a lovely terraced house with four bedrooms, two reception rooms, a kitchen and a lovely bathroom with shower. We met the owners, Basil and his wife, Mary; we liked each other straight away. They have been great friends of ours ever since.

I love this little town. It has a central square with seats and flower beds all around it. There are lots of little shops, which have a Dickensian air about them. A supermarket is very nearby, a library, a few primary schools and a comprehensive school.

One of the good things about Barnoldswick is that there are no main roads going through it, so cars and lorries are just coming to Barnoldswick, which keeps the amount of traffic down.

There is a very good surgery with about six doctors working in it, and some nursing staff; they are all very helpful. A town bus travels all over the town every half an hour, and there are taxis available. The supermarket delivers groceries free of charge, and the chemist will deliver prescriptions, so we elderly folk are very well taken care of.

There are two parks, one with lovely views over the town and hills around. A canal goes through the town and is close to where we live now. It's nice to walk along the canal and see the swans and ducks, and watch the narrow boats coming along and people waving to us.

Our friends Dennis and Val now live in York, which is about an hour and a half away. They often come to visit us and sometimes I stay with them for a few days. Dennis has retired from television now, and spends his retirement gardening, cooking and using his computer. He also takes wonderful photographs. After Val stopped work as a full time make-up artist, she taught make-up at York College. They are very special friends and always come to any family events we have like weddings, birthdays, Sue's 50th birthday and our Golden Wedding event, to which all my children, grandchildren and great grandchildren came.

After we bought Basil and Mary's house, they moved to a smaller house about eight houses away. Pete and I used to have evenings with them, playing cards and Mah Jong. We spent New Year and Christmas together sometimes. They have both spent some time at an ashram in India with a well known spiritual master. Mary had to go into a mental hospital for a while with bi-polar disorder, so we share lots of our experiences together, as we understand each other.

Sadly Basil died a few years ago, which was devastating for Mary and sad for us. Mary is my very special friend.

My dear friend Carol moved to Barnoldswick and we are still good friends. I used to see a lot of her, but we didn't see much of each other after I was ill, for about six years, as I didn't want to see anyone very much. She is a very talented woman who has run her own fancy dress business, which expanded into a costume hire company, with thousands of costumes for the theatre.

She has been a hypnotherapist and still practises her healing; she's also a drama teacher at the local comprehensive. She spends a lot of her time now travelling with her husband all over the world as part of his job. We still get together occasionally, and we share a love of books and exploring spirituality, especially within ourselves. I remember spending one of my birthdays with Val, Carol and Mary when we went to a pub in the country near here for a lovely meal.

I have a good friendship with Julia, my sister-in-law, a lovely woman who lives with her husband Peter in Kent; I am very fond of her. She has three children and five grandchildren. They come to see Peter and I two or three times a year. I love Bob and Doreen who are Peter's brother and his wife. They still live in Launceston and keep in touch by phone two or three times a week. They have been to see us occasionally, but we are a long way from Cornwall and it's not easy for us to meet up very often. They are lovely people, with two grown up sons. Peter had a younger brother called John, who lived in Australia and sadly died a few years ago. It was a very sad time for all of us. His wife Marian still keeps in touch and they have three grown up sons.

So, as you can see, I belong to a very large group of family and friends, for which I feel very blessed, but I do enjoy my own company and the silence of meditation and contemplation of Life.

I went to see my doctor as I was in pain. He examined me and said I had fibroids, so he suggested I have a hysterectomy. I went to see a specialist in our local hospital and after he had examined me he said I definitely needed a hysterectomy. He said he would be doing the operation, and as we were in BUPA, it would be done at Gisburn Park Hospital, just a few miles from Barnoldswick. Because this is the kind of thing I do, I asked him if I could put my hands on his head, to see if he was the right person to do the operation. He smiled and said, "Yes, of course, if that helps you." He felt like a kind and caring man, so I said, "You will be fine to do the operation."

A few weeks later I went into Gisburn Park Hospital, and had the operation. Everything went very well and I made a rapid recovery. The consultant said he had to come and see me, as I had made such a good recovery. I soon went back home with Pete and felt fine in a few weeks.

A VERY BRIEF INTERLUDE

When I was 39, I decided to go to College, to take my O level English and A level English and Communication. I was hoping to one day go to university. I met my O level English teacher and we got on very well. Then he introduced me to Michael, my A level English and Communication teacher. I don't remember what he said to me but I was mesmerized by his voice. Every lesson with Michael was magical after that and I was totally smitten. A few weeks later during lessons, the class planned a three day trip to London to go to theatres and television studios to study Communication.

The first evening we were in London, Michael and I had dinner together, as I was the only mature student. Then later, at bedtime, he came to my room and we made love. It lasted about five minutes and was pretty useless, compared with Peter. I knew it wasn't sex I wanted, I just wanted to hear his voice, which I had fallen in love with. His wife arrived the following day, so we had no more time together and when the three days were over, we all travelled back home on the train.

Pete was waiting for me at the station, with a buttonhole in his lapel. I will never forget how terrible I felt when I saw him. A few days later, I told him what had happened and he said, "Perhaps you are not happy with me."

That was not true, but when I returned to College and to Michael's lessons, the effect of his voice still churned my stomach. I stayed at College until I had an A in my O level English and then I left for good and knew I had ruined my dream of going to university. Pete forgave me and I forgot Michael eventually, but I still wonder how it is possible to love someone because of the sound of his voice?

We lived in our lovely terraced house for many years and a lot happened in the family. Helen married John, and they had a daughter and a son. Sue and Henry managed to get a house near the canal and have two daughters and a son. Steve married Kate and they lived in Barnoldswick a few years and had two sons. Jeremy was still at home during my illness but later married Sarah and they have two sons and a daughter. Lucy was still at home and moved house with us.

The schizophrenia happened before we left our terraced house, when I was 43 years old. Jeremy was about fifteen and Lucy was twelve. It was so hard for Peter and our children to go through this experience, which I am sure has affected them all.

6 FIVE BEAUTIFUL CHILDREN

Helen, Suzanne, Steve, Jeremy and Lucy are very important to me, as our children are to most people. They are also individual souls that chose us to be their parents and we have a duty to guide them as they begin their Path through Life. It's not easy to be a parent and however hard we try, none of us are perfect. If we have done the best we can, in spite of the wounds we may carry from our own childhood, then no more can be asked of us.

I love my children dearly, as does Pete, and this is the most precious and probably the only thing we can truly give. I hope you will enjoy the poems I have written about each one of them, as they paint a picture of five very individual people who are, like all of us, treading the fascinating Journey of Life.

I am blessed by them, with twelve grandchildren and seven great grandchildren, who bring so much joy into my life.

HELEN

To speak to your heart, dear daughter,
Is not an easy thing.
The arrow once sped, goes where it will
And I cannot follow.

I feel so proud of the woman you've become.
Why should I feel pride? You did it by yourself.
Long days and nights of study to reach your goal
And two children to raise, with only a little help.

Like me, you have a secret heart
That God gives to everyone.
In it, I know, is your love for Humanity
And the Honesty that comes from the soul.

The pupils must be glad you are their teacher.
I wonder what they would say if they were aware
You once saw auras and nature spirits
And had a secret friend that none saw.

There never was a need to say "I'm sorry."
Better far if I had said it to you
When I was neglectful of my duty as your mum,
So busy having other things to do.

You have known love and separation sometimes,
Faced it all with courage and with hope.
Not to say you were never afraid
You just said, "I can do this," and you did.

He knows how hard you struggle.
He cares that you always try.
He taught me how to love you.
For you are a very special woman

SUZANNE

My dearest daughter, born into my youth,
These words are sent to light your way,
Maybe to a brighter path to tread
With every brand new day.

I see it all within you.
You shine with a special light
Of caring and compassion to us all.
Yet I remember, you have paid a heavy price.

Recall a child filled with sunlight
With a smile for who you met.
Sue is such a happy child, they said;
Even strangers in a café didn't forget.

You grew into a woman, so beautiful to see,
An artist's touch into your hand, as a gift
For all to treasure and understand, that
Not all artists are painters, but so free.

You know the suffering of your fellow man
And do everything within your power
To heal it and to mend, and people come
To warm themselves in your light.

You have three lovely children,
A husband as kind as can be.
Though problems are many, you still carry on
With a faith that is easy to see.

I have caused you some pain and worry
When insanity threatened my life.
For this I am sorry, not wanting it so.
Just glad it seems past for a while.

It often is good to make changes,
To leave all the pain in the past.
Set out on a beautiful journey
Freeing the secret heart, at last.

STEVE

Memories of Hallatrow
Haunt this October day
When you drove a pedal car
And visited my café.

Now you are a man, my Son,
Living an island life, not far away,
And walk the hills, or watch the sea
As I wonder what your thoughts may be.

You've had a charmed life it seems,
Touching everyone you meet
With your kindness, laughter and gentle ways.
A free spirit that's hard to restrain.

A loving wife, two grown up sons,
Create your family home.
You always do your best for them
But like each one of us, you walk alone.

Sporting triumphs cannot be left untold
They hold a special place,
Whether football, cricket or golf,
Or throwing a javelin such a long way.

I worry about the pain you suffered
When I became ill and unable to care.
I could have gone forever, but Love smiled
And said, "It's only for a moment, don't despair."

So here we all are, on this Journey of Life,
Treading each step of the way.
May Love go with you, as you travel along,
And Sunshine be there every day.

He doesn't expect much from us Travellers,
Just a heart that is eager to learn
Of Truth and Beauty, or a drop of rain,
Falling in the Ocean of Time, again and again.

He gave me and your father

The gift of a wonderful son.
We are so proud of what you have achieved.
God bless you, dear Steve - It's done.

JEREMY

You came with a smile upon your face
Before you even woke each morning.
Were you thinking of another land unseen
Or was it just the memory of a dream?

Let's pass over the difficult years
We journeyed through together.
A sensitive soul finds it difficult to grow
And how hard you struggled, we will never know.

Your loving heart and sense of fun,
Just caring for us all each day
Lit a light for you, within our hearts
That we can never repay.

You and your lovely wife have been blessed
With two sons and a daughter so fair
And you work so hard for all of them,
To prove how much you love and care.

Trials and troubles have come your way
As they do to us all, now and then
But your heart has been strong, you still carry on,
With His help, every step of the way.

When illness overwhelmed me
I could count on your loving support,
Which you gave as often as you could,
Not just like a passing thought

He watches over each one of us,
He'll catch us when we fall,
So may He always be part of your life,
Dear Jeremy, for now, that's all.

LUCY

Lucy is a Star in my life.
She could be one to you
With love in her heart, for everyone,
She won't mind an extra one or two.

The youngest of our children,
You have a special place
With your fun-loving ways, and big blue eyes
And the laughter, which we all embrace.

You have the gift of an artist;
Some of your paintings are in my room,
Gifts I treasure and gaze at
When I feel lonely, or full of gloom.

The great joy in your life is your wonderful son;
I remember the day he was born,
Saw you emerge, an amazing mum
Watching over him as he grew.

You became a competent gardener,
Following your father's ways
With an inner love for Nature
And many gardens in which to spend your days.

You've known some pain and sorrow
But you would be first to admit
It was always that you loved too well;
They didn't ever hear your song
Or the story you had to tell.

We all make mistakes on our Journey
But He loves us, in spite of our faults
And all He asks is a loving heart
That we carry on our journey to the Stars.

Be kind to yourself, dearest daughter,
May a rainbow colour your day,
For my love will surround you always
As you walk on your beautiful way.

Now you have another son
Dear Wolfie has come, with his fun,
Youngest of my grandchildren, bless him.
I think he brought the sparkle of the Sun.

7 A SPECIAL LADY

Into your jewelled presence
I came that sunny day,
Saw the varicose veins on your legs
And knew I loved you,
Entered your wonderful world,
While you held the key on a lilac ribbon.
Just a terraced house to some, but to me
A monastery, where every room was filled
With delights, special things that held
An energy of their own, and work for me to do.

I could not stay away from you for long,
Trod the path to your door, on winged feet
Knocked on the door, would you answer?
Like an angel from another land.
I brought you flowers; we shared a cup of tea
Heart to heart, your wisdom spoke
To my untutored self and I would find a trinket
That you explained, and so I took another step.

So filled with love for you, I sang at your door
Sometimes we travelled together, to a café,
A jumble sale or on a bus.
The light in you touched everything around
And I walked like one in a dream.

Carried the coal to light your fire,
Served tea to your visitors,
Painted a wall blue, with a tiny tin of paint
And a two inch paintbrush,
Sorted out a pile of many coloured wool;
What I couldn't separate, you threw into the fire.

In my secret heart, the love we shared
And the teaching you gave me, lives on.
The last time I saw you, your body
Stricken by strokes, I thought you were lost
to me. But as I was about to leave
Your face turned to me and your blue eyes
Forever young, gazed into mine and I knew
The joy of Love, not forgotten.

My story would not be complete without mention of Lily. She came into my life in this little town before I was ill. Lily has now passed on, but she played a great part in my life.

It's quite funny how we met; I'd just gone for a walk with my friend, Carol, when we came to a little basement shop which was shut. I said to Carol, "I know we've got to wait here and someone will come and let us in." Sure enough Lily turned up.

She was an old lady with dreamy blue eyes. "Were you waiting for me," she said and opened the door and let us in. It was like Aladdin's cave, everywhere piled high with pottery ornaments, cups, saucers, plates and trinkets. Even though it was so shambolic, there seemed to be a pattern in it all that seemed to make sense to me. I didn't want to be anywhere else.

One day I came to visit her by myself and she let me into her home. I was very surprised to find her home very much like her shop, every room filled with piles of things. Yet there was always enough room to move and sit down. If she broke anything, she would look at it and say, "Well, if that's what you want to do, off you go." She kept a few sachets of coffee and tea bags to make a drink with. One day, her daughter, who lived a few doors away, brought us a cooked meal which we ate together. It was almost as if she didn't really live there, like she just appeared.

We travelled by bus one day, to visit a market in a large town near us. It was a magical day. When she was picking out something from a stall, she would take quite a while before she chose what to buy, and every item had a special quality. We went for coffee and a cake then came home on the bus. She seemed to know quite a few people on the bus and chatted to them all.

A young couple came to the shop one day. Lily only opened the shop on certain occasions. She asked me to go upstairs and make them tea, but it had to be in black and white china cups. Well, there were so many cups that I had no problem finding the right ones.

When it was Christmas time, she came to my house with a gift for me. It was an oil lamp with two galleons painted on the shade. I was very surprised when she came to my home, as I had never told her my surname or my address and I lived on the other side of town. I used to light the lamp a lot, until one day I couldn't find it anywhere. This would happen to a lot of the things I bought from her; she always charged me 75 pence for anything I purchased.

I do not have anything left of the things I bought from her; they have all vanished over the last few years.

She certainly had an effect on my life, during the long time I visited her. If I were to ask myself, "What is a teacher?" I would say that Lily was a teacher for me. I think that all over the world there are people like Lily, who turn up in our lives, at various times, to help us understand about life, relationships, and also what we need to learn. I took people that I knew to meet her. They thought she was a very strange lady but never saw her the way I did. They were affected by her and felt she was different from a lot of people.

I can't really talk about what she taught me and the love she gave to me. All I can say is that she gave me clues on how to behave, how to see things in a different way. Little did I know that when I eventually suffered from schizophrenia and had the strange experiences that come with this illness, she had given me a picture of what it would be like, and how to deal with altered states of mind.

So for this I thank her, wherever she is, and I will never forget her.

8 SCHIZOPHRENIA

I have an illness, it has a name,
Yet no two people who have it are the same
And all those who haven't got it
Are afraid of the name of it.

All except you, dear Lord.
You allow us to be part of your Creation
And your Love surrounds us,
Just as it does everyone.

Most of us live in a shadow world
And we carry the fears of men.
Voices speak to us from the Stars
Medication, music and cigarettes are my crutch.

For thirty years, I have run from this label,
Denying it's reality out of fear.
But I will not be afraid anymore.
So I say to the World, I am a schizophrenic.

Joan.

The First Journey

It took place in 1985, when I was 43 years old.

It was just an ordinary day; I had been feeling a bit tense, but that was all. Lots of people came to see me that day, friends and family. My sister Rachael came from Devon to stay for a few days. Everything started to get a bit strange. I decided that what I lay out for tea had to be yellow; yellow cake, yellow candles and yellow flowers.

In the afternoon I began to feel odd, very tall, almost like a giant. People around me looked strange, their faces altered and we all became like actors in a play. I was playing music non-stop, one thing after another, which seemed to intensify the mood.

After tea, my sister and I watched two films, "Finian's Rainbow" and "The Colour Purple." Even the television was strange; everything that was happening on the screen seemed related to me and my sister in some way. Rachael and I have watched these films again over the years, and she always says they are just not the same as they were that evening so long ago. It was as if they connected with some fantastic journey I was experiencing.

After watching the films my sister and I decided to go for a walk into Barnoldswick centre. The people we met on the journey to town all looked more alive and sparkling. All the shops were lit up and it seemed like a magical place. Everyone spoke to us, or at least it felt like that. There was a picture framing shop full of lights and the little man who owned it opened the door and said "Would you like to look around?" It was after closing time so it seemed a bit odd. I looked at all the pictures and they had special meanings for me, connecting to the idea of a journey.

Rachael and I walked home and spent the evening playing games with the family. Gradually everyone drifted off to bed but I stayed up as I was wide awake and experiencing powerful connections with all the things around me, and dancing to music till 1 a.m. Looking out of the window, I was aware of a face watching me; it was the face of a very wise man. I said to him, "I'll do anything you wish". There were tears in his eyes as I looked at him and I felt the tears were for me, but I wondered why, when I felt so happy.

The happiness with life reached such a pitch that I was overwhelmed. It was then that a strange figure entered the room. He was wearing a dark cloak but I wasn't afraid of him, even though I felt in my heart that he was the Angel of Death. I cannot remember what he said to me, I just remember saying "Surely I can hang on to a cup of coffee and a cigarette."

He left and I went to bed but instead of sleeping, I had the experience of travelling out into space as part of the universe. I heard a voice saying "Have you got her?" and another voice answering "Yes, she's quite safe." I was imprisoned in a golden cage and that was the last I knew for six days.

Many things happened during those six days that I knew nothing of. I was much later told by Pete that I had thrown myself down the stairs, and he had saved me. Doctors came to see me and Pete, Steve and John, my son-in-law, had to hold me down while I was given injections, none of which seemed to have any effect. I apparently boiled kettles and flicked the boiling water around the room. In the end an ambulance came about 3 a.m. a couple of days later. I was out in the street saying, "I don't want to get in that space machine." All of this was unknown to me; this is just what I have been told.

I was taken to the mental ward of a local hospital. Peter was so horrified at my treatment there that after two days, with me still unconscious, he had me transferred to a private hospital in Manchester as he was in BUPA. Four days later I woke up.

It was very pink, pink walls and a pink bathroom attached. I thought I had died and gone to Heaven. I staggered into the bathroom and looked in the mirror but was horrified to see the face of a very old woman. I went out of the bedroom, onto the landing, where there was a table, two armchairs and a bench. There was a nurse sitting in one of the chairs. I went into the kitchen and made myself a cup of coffee, sat on the bench and lit a cigarette, which Peter had left for me.

Then the terrible truth dawned on me; I was alive and in some strange place. I thought it was a different land; somehow I had got into another world.

Then I felt the rejection, a rejection from God. I thought, "God has rejected me. I died and have been thrown back. I'm not good enough." I didn't want to see my family or friends, only Peter.

Peter came every night after work to visit me, except Saturday. So began a long painful suffering. Weeping for the fact that I hadn't proved adequate enough as a person to be accepted, the feeling of rejection was paramount.

The kitchen was just off the landing and coffee, milk and sugar were provided twenty four hours a day. I spent the next two months on this landing. Later I wandered round the hospital, past bedrooms and up and down the stairs, saying nothing and weeping all the time, always looking for an answer, to find acceptance somewhere for the loss I felt. Nurses were kind and did their best, but I was lost.

A pigeon used to land outside my bedroom window and I talked to him and would send messages to Peter. I felt sure the pigeon would take the messages. My room was very sparse. I even turned the mirror around, not to see the pain in my face. I longed for the time in the evening when Peter came; these were very precious times. I believed Peter had some special ability to be able to visit my world, and that was why I was able to see him. I clung to him as my only contact with my family in that other world, that seemed so far away.

It was in this hospital that I first met Dr M. I could do very little when I first saw him, except ramble; I was engulfed in flames, I was crucified on a cross. I talked to him of the little town where I lived that was so full of light and sparkling. He listened very patiently.

There in that hospital I stayed for eight months. After about three or four months the weeping gradually subsided. I still didn't join in with the others, and my meals were sent up to the landing, plates of sandwiches of which I ate very little. I had a tapestry that Peter brought in for me to do. It was a brass rubbing of a medieval saint, very difficult, brown wool and gold thread. I started it while I sat on the landing and somehow concentrating on it helped.

One day I decided to go to Occupational Therapy. I was very frightened as I went in. Lots of people were there, sewing, making cakes and producing amazing collages. I sat down on a chair; someone made me a cup of coffee. I did a few stitches of my tapestry but then I had to get up and leave, but it was a first step.

After that I went and sat in the lounge. The other patients were sitting in armchairs, some smoking, some drinking tea or coffee. Gradually I began to say hello and people started to speak to me. There was a quiet room where jigsaws were done, so one day I went and did a jigsaw.

I remember a door in the quiet room that seemed to lead nowhere, and from the open door I could hear the voice of Kathleen Ferrier singing, "Blow thou wind southerly." I wanted to go through that door but I was afraid that if I went, I would never get back.

So I carried on walking around the hospital, waiting for Peter's visit. He didn't come on a Saturday, as that was his day for cleaning the house, cooking meals and spending time with the youngest two of our children, who were still at home. I watched the squirrels playing in the garden; it seemed I could talk to them better than I could the people around me.

My Psychiatrist, Dr M, told me my schizophrenia was not hereditary and also that my illness had additional aspects to the Schizophrenia.

So, I was happy to know that my children and their offspring would not be affected by this condition. For six months Dr M tried various drugs. I also had three sessions of E.C.T. none of which seemed to do me a lot of good, although I was becoming more confident. Finally Dr M put me on an injection called Redeptin, which seemed after forty eight hours to have an amazing effect. For the first time I went to the dining room for a meal. After that I used to go down for meals every day. At last Dr M said I was well enough to go home for the weekend.

I couldn't believe that I was able to travel from this world to my own world. I was very quiet all the way home, so pleased to see the children; I cried a lot. They were quite grown up now, both teenagers, my lovely Jeremy and Lucy. Peter made a meal but I couldn't eat much. I managed to get through the weekend; it was so wonderful to be home.

So my time in that hospital came to an end and I was sent home for good. I thought I was cured and well after an unusual experience. For the next four years a lot of my time was spent sitting in a chair reading cheap romantic novels; if anyone asked me I would say, "I'm convalescing." Sadly this was not to be the end of my experiences, but in spite of what I had yet to experience, I don't think any journey was as bad as this first one.

Three invisible "Doctors"

Four years after my first illness, I became aware of my three doctors. I was in my bedroom at home one day, making my bed. One of them spoke to me and asked me to lie on the bed and stay very still. They were going to put a receiver in my brain and also strengthen my body. I lay on the bed and was aware of a hum all around me and a bright light entering my forehead. After this I went downstairs. I thought, "Well, that was a bit strange," but I often had strange things happening to me, so I didn't bother about it very much. I put classic F.M. on the radio to listen to some music and then I was aware of them again. One of them said, "We want to see how much pain you can stand but don't worry, we won't make it too much for you to bear." About five minutes after this I felt the pain begin in my body until it increased to an almost unbearable level. They seemed pleased with this, then before they left, said "Try not to worry; we'll always be there to help you."

They didn't come to see me again until I had a relapse and went to our local hospital mental ward, when they were with me and helped me to survive the ordeals I had to face. I was burnt at the stake as a witch and felt the flames. I was stoned to death by a crowd of faceless people and felt the pain. At times I was in so much pain; it was almost more than I could bear.

I was aware all the time of my three unseen doctors who healed the pain and suffering I endured and also seemed to be altering my brain chemistry. They made it possible for me to survive the experiences I had and return to so-called normality. Yet through all these times my three doctors felt more real than what we call reality, and I will never forget them.

Even though I no longer see them, I know that they have taken a part of me with them, back to the star that they came from. Perhaps one day I will join them. I watched them leave this world one evening a few years ago and have not seen them since. This sequence of events may seem a little bizarre, but they were as real to me as anyone I might meet in the street. They were gentle and kind and gave me the love and care that I never had from any living doctor, psychiatrist or mental nurse. When I wept, they comforted me and in all I did they guided my steps. I called them my three doctors because that is how I saw them.

The episodes of schizophrenia at times can be very frightening, and also very painful. Your vision is constantly bombarded with even the most insignificant events, like eating a meal or walking around the ward. A potted plant or a picture on T.V. can have a traumatic effect, so the support of these "doctors" was absolutely essential to my sanity, as the world was very strange to me in those times. What they did more than anything else was to make me realise that God had never rejected me but had actually given me back my life and would always love me as He does everyone.

Episodes of Schizophrenia

Because of the experiences I have had over the last thirty years, I feel I no longer fit into this world. I am a stranger in a strange land. They say I have schizophrenia, but at the end of the day it's only a word that can apply to lots of people with very different experiences to mine. In one experience I became a whale and carried a hundred people in my belly; they were all the people I had ever known in my life. I made a journey, as this whale, across the sea to an island. It was a very long and arduous trip and I had to be pulled ashore with ropes as I ended the journey and everyone stepped out of me onto the island. Ever since this time I have loved the sound of whales and feel they understand much more about Man's destiny than we realise.

All the experiences I have had over five or six relapses since my first episode have given me a different view of the world. When I'm not having a relapse, I live a fairly normal life, with the occasional difficult day surrounded by my large family. They have also suffered, watching me go through these episodes, and they have seen many things that I was unaware of. They did not see what I saw and this makes me sad, to know how much they suffered. Sufferers of schizophrenia are in another world and while I was in this world, I felt that other patients, nurses and visitors were also in my world and could see what I could see.

I think it is worth mentioning that in all the thirty years I have had this illness, no psychiatrist or mental nurse has ever asked me what I was experiencing, and this could have helped a lot. They just treated the psychotic behaviour with massive amounts of drugs, many of which I was allergic to. They never eased the "Journey" I was on; that came to an end overnight, when the "Journey" was finished.

I feel this treatment was very often a failing by the medical people, who could not relate to us at all. If we get better, it is often because of our own work within ourselves. I do not want to be this way or have this illness, but I would like to think of it as an altered state of consciousness and heightened awareness. During these episodes we need to be kept safe, but there must be a better way than mental wards in a hospital, where one is locked in and subject to the hospital's rules and regulations.

Living a Dark Day

Woke at 4 a.m., feeling very disoriented; my head was feeling twice the normal size and I was crying a lot. Put on some music and lit a candle. I rang the Crisis Team, as they are available twenty four hours a day, to let them know how I felt. Went to bed at 11 a.m., after sitting in the garden, and slept a little while. Went downstairs feeling numb and exhausted. Couldn't do very much. At 7 p.m. I went to bed as my head was not functioning at all. Did not want to see or speak to anyone, except Pete. Took two Diazipam at 11 p.m. and slept on and off till 4 a.m. Got up and went down to the kitchen, dried dishes, tidied kitchen, washed my hair and played some music. Felt awful, with pains in my head, took two Paracetamol and went back to bed at 10 a.m.

Went downstairs again at 11 a.m. after no sleep since 4 a.m. and it's now 3 p.m. and I don't know what I have been doing, this often happens when I have times like this. I'm listening to John Denver singing, in my bedroom, wondering where I am. I slept for two hours then went down to the kitchen for some soup and a glass of water. Stayed down for a while, then went back to bed and slept another couple of hours. Now down in the kitchen, its 2 a.m. and at last I can feel some peace. I don't mind Pete being with me. He never intrudes in times like these.

Pete has gone to bed now and I am listening to Nick Drake singing, having a cup of coffee. I have been through so much and this is the first time since last year I have felt a little space for myself. I am just being carried along and only able to connect in a limited way. Whatever this is, I think I'll be able to manage without the Crisis Team at the moment; we shall see. The grief over my mum's passing seems to have eased, the concern over my grandaughters serious illness has also improved and I have done all I can for my neighbour, so here I am, waiting for whatever this is. Three a.m., listening to Cat Stevens singing, washing done, waiting for daylight to hang it on the line. I have been looking at a book that our friend Phil sent - pictures of Stars and Galaxies. They are so beautiful. Needed the Crisis Team for a week, but things gradually eased with help from my doctor, the Crisis Team and my Community Psychiatric Nurse.

This road of Life is so long, and I have struggled so many years. Yes, the Crisis Team may help but I am at the mercy of this crazy world that has rules on how to treat people like me, and will not accept that we have dark times, and the world can seem very hostile and uncaring.

Why should they be surprised that I turn to you, dear Lord, at times like this and let you lead me along a road that has become too difficult for a while? The night goes on and I have let go, just moving along life's path, wherever it leads. I will sleep, when I can, and meanwhile, just enjoy the night. May the Light, that forever shines, spread over this poor world and light up the darkness.

TURMOIL

We all want to help you, they cry,
Cope with the depression,
Handle the mood swings
And give you support.

I follow their advice,
Do as they ask,
Take their pills and potions,
Yet still pace the kitchen in the night.

But from my secret heart
A voice whispers "hold tight"
Protect the light and journey on;
Only the frailty of your body captures their mind.

When I least expect it, my Master draws near
Talking of age old wisdom and secret teaching.
Then I remember what I have learnt
And the turmoil subsides.

Joan.

Relapse

Ever since I have had this illness, I never know when I am about to have a relapse until a few days before I am taken into hospital. I wake up one morning and feel different from my usual self. I can feel energy in the air, colours seem brighter and I find myself concentrating on everything that happens in the day, what is said and what I do. If I travel on the bus into town, the journey seems important; the supermarket is alive and glowing. It is extremely difficult to explain what I see. It has been likened to being on drugs, but apart from the medication I have had in hospital, I have never taken mind-altering drugs, so I don't know if this is true.

I once went out of my home in nightdress and dressing gown in the pouring rain, stopping a car and telling them what a lovely day it was. My neighbour took me back home. After this, Peter kept the back door locked in case I wandered off again. My Community Psychiatric Nurse came to see me and suggested I go into hospital. Being no longer able to afford a private hospital, I went into the mental ward of my local hospital. Often, when I had a relapse and was taken into hospital, I would become unconscious for a period of time, so I wouldn't remember the journey to the ward. I spent six weeks or sometimes six months in hospital depending on the length of time I was in my strange world. Then I would wake up one morning and the relapse was over and I was back to myself.

Most of my time was spent interacting with other patients, as the nursing staff were not able to relate to us and left us very much to ourselves. The patients became part of my experience; there was one that I saw as the Devil, another as a saint. We were all very sick and yet we understood one another and took care of each other.

If only someone let us talk about what we were experiencing, it could have helped us a great deal. Of course, everyone's experience is different, and perhaps the nurses didn't have time to listen to us. It seems sad that people suffering from schizophrenia, should be left to experience the traumas that go with this illness alone. Yes, they filled us full of drugs, most of which I was allergic to and none of which stopped the experiences I had. No one will ever know how many nights I cried myself to sleep. It wasn't all painful; we used to laugh a lot with each other and even dance at times.

I had M.R.I. scans and brain scans and my psychiatrist told me that all they had discovered was that I had one brainwave that was different from most people's. Was this the cause? I shall never know. On average I had a relapse every three or four years. The last one was in 2009 and I haven't had another one since; as I write it is 2015.

The last relapse began before I was taken into hospital again. I was feeling so well, I'd lost some weight and was busy writing a study of North American Indian Spirituality, which I found fascinating. I stayed awake at night making notes in my journal. In the day I would travel on the bus into town to meet up with friends and advise them on their health problems. I had learnt a lot about natural cures in my studies and wanted to help others.

It was about this time that my perception changed. Everywhere became much sharper and more alive. One day a mobile office arrived in the Central Square of the town, manned by half a dozen people giving out information to the public on the new T.V. reception that was coming. They looked like aliens to me; they had a television mast on top of their van, which I thought was some kind of communication device. They handed out free pens to anyone that stopped to speak to them. I refused to have one as I didn't know what these pens were for.

I would catch the bus at 9.00 a.m. to travel to town and often didn't go home till 4.00 p.m. All this became too much for Peter to cope with, so he called in the Crisis Team. The Crisis Team visits people with mental health problems and tries to prevent them having to go into hospital. They came to talk to me as I wasn't sleeping very much and Peter and my daughter, Sue, were worried. It was decided that I would go for a rest in a special convalescent home for a short period of time. I went with the Crisis Team, but only stayed for a few days as I became worse and was transferred to my usual hospital ward.

I have no idea how I got there as I was unconscious and I don't know how long it was before I became aware of my surroundings. I felt my first task was to heal the patients around me. There were three jugs containing water, orange and lemon juice, so I made it my job to fill these whenever they were empty. I believed that all the patients had died and arrived in the ward to be revived. I watched over them all very carefully, and did everything I could to help them adjust to being there and get better. I didn't feel I belonged there, but that I was on a healing mission to help these poor souls.

I made tea and coffee for them from the trolley and was very loving when they were in pain or distressed. We became like a close-knit family, sharing everything. Nurses came and went, took us out for a smoke or a walk to a nearby park. My life became a dream world, and the weeks and months went by very quickly. We danced to music in the lounge, waved to people passing by the window and to the staff in the office, who we could see through a window as they sat at their computers.

I remember I looked out of my bedroom window one night and saw a winter tree covered in the most beautiful lilac blossom. Later I was aware that some of the patients, nurses and visitors seemed to be from another planet. It then became a kind of battle between the normal people and the aliens. I said to one visitor, "Why are you here?" He said, "We thought you needed some help." I said, "No, we don't, so go back to the planet you came from." The "Battle" went on with everyone taking different roles, until one day I was downstairs in the entrance, where we used to smoke, when I saw a spaceship leave, with blue lights, until the lights went orange and white and it became an ordinary aeroplane that flew away.

One day I went for a meeting with Dr B, my psychiatrist, and a few other people. I told him he had been sick but was getting better. He said I would be able to go home soon, but when we had our next meeting he said he had no memory of our previous meeting and had not told me I could go home. It was all very strange. I spent six months in the ward, and as usual just woke up one morning and I was back to normal. I spent a few days sleeping and was then allowed to go home. It was Christmas and snow was on the ground. I was very happy to be back with my family.

9 TALKING TO GOD

These are some of the entries I made daily, over the last thirty years, in journals entitled "Talking to God." They helped a great deal. I have not included the prayers for family and friends, as they are private. You may wish to do something similar. If you have a problem with using the word God, you can pick something else, like Great Spirit, or Soul of the Universe. I'm sure God doesn't mind what you call him.

*

Where are You my Lord, hidden from my sight like roots in the Earth? Alone in this alien land I walk unseen.

*

Tender-hearted children call to me, "Hello, Nanny." What am I to answer? Just a kindly word for souls that tread Your Path. I will one day be far away and yet my heart will hold them dear.

*

Touch my soul, my Lord, my life. Turn my speech into silence in wonder of You. May Your Light be with us all and may we grow ever nearer to You.

*

It's funny, when I am talking to You dear Lord, all the cares of the day seem to disappear and I feel almost like a child again, without a care, when You are there.

*

The days come and go, and yet I seem unable to improve myself in any way. What do You want of us dear Lord? May I, at least, become content with my own company? I seem to be always phoning someone, so I don't have to feel the aloneness. What is it that I am afraid of? That my life will seem a waste of time in the great scheme of things? If I have a higher self, may I discover how to reach it and the guidance I need to fulfil my life's

73

purpose? I have felt this Higher Connection when it seems I have something to do, then it goes and I am all at sea again.

*

If I could have one wish, dear Lord, it would be to feel again the joy I felt before I was "ill".

*

I stay here, dear Lord, day after day, seeming to do nothing. If I can do anything, please show me in what direction to move. I drink wine to sleep, I take sleeping tablets to sleep, all seemingly to shorten the waiting time, and yet, what am I waiting for?

*

I am sitting in the beautiful garden that Peter has made, and the noise and bustle of life goes on around me.

*

May I, in an instant, rise from time and space. Set the world aside and become a world within myself.

*

Thank You for the love I feel from Peter and for keeping us together through all the difficult times.

*

I must just tell You about the wonderful garden Peter has created; it is a real expression of Love for You and Your works. It feels so special, just to walk around and see so much beauty and feel such a healing atmosphere.

*

I keep thinking of all the joy and happiness I used to feel about life, and wonder if I shall ever feel this again. So much pain and tears, the path seems far away and I can't feel Your love or guidance. Please forgive me.

*

I realise that I have a lot of fear about everyday life, which I never used to have. All I can do is ask You to help me overcome this fear.

*

Many weeks have passed, coping with illness, but I begin to see a light. As I do, I humbly ask that I may be allowed to travel on my spiritual journey. This is where I belong, sitting at my table thinking of You and trying to speak with You from the heart.

A difficult illness

A virus, like an alien invader, laid me low.
Fever, pain, sweating, sleepless nights,
All came to me in six long weeks.
Have I lost You, dear Lord?

Did You wish me to experience this illness?
To learn the frailty of Man and Woman.
I tried to continue listening to Your teaching
But it was not easy and I failed a lot.

These last few days I'm feeling better
Yet almost afraid to be well.
What did I use to do, before this?
Did I have a purpose, or a Path to tread?

This strange in-between time of recovery,
Wanting to make a new beginning,
To try harder, to make fewer mistakes,
To be grateful for the healing, and carry on.

*

May we learn kindness, humility and compassion for people we meet,
and may we grow in Love for our nearest and dearest. Bless all the children
of the World, and ease the suffering of those less fortunate than us.

*

Sometimes I think that if I sit here at my table long enough, I will be
able to understand what we are supposed to do in this life we have been
given. It doesn't seem to work like that, for after a while I get thirsty and
make a drink, eat something or smoke a cigarette and so the time passes. I
remember all the time I spent in hospital, heartbroken and soul searching,
and yet always the Truth seemed to elude me. Somewhere, I was aware of
Your Love for us all and that was why I recovered and am still able to talk
to You.

*

I have a heart that longs to please my Lord, if I knew how, but my mind
is damaged and seems only able to make very small steps along the way.
After a year, with six months of it spent in a mental hospital, and being seen
as a sick woman, I have emerged back into the light, to carry on my spiritual
journey. Some of my family, psychiatrists and nurses, think that my books
by a great Spiritual Teacher caused my illness. In fact, these books saved me

from a far worse fate. My illness was caused, I believe, by my childhood and the overwhelming fear I experienced then.

*

I have always thought that I was a loving person but now I wonder if this is true. Do I still love people when they criticise or attack me? It's not an easy thing to love Humanity, almost impossible. It's said you cannot love others if you do not love yourself, but I can love myself, for in God's Light, I am not worthless.

*

Peter and I seem to be living separate lives at present. It's so sad; we have so little time. I seem to have lost the art of conversation, spending most of my days in silence; it must be difficult for him to deal with. The pain and longing in my heart grows ever stronger and there is no-one who would understand it, except You dear Lord.

*

I need to stop treating Peter as if he were my father, always doing what he wants me to, and trying to avoid arguments or confrontations. He didn't ask to be put in the role of father or boss figure. I always shrink when he appears and watch his every move and everything he says - how stupid! When did this start to happen? After I came home from hospital in 2009 I think. I'm sure Pete doesn't want this, any more than I do. So I must be very aware of what happens, and try and lose the ghost of my father for the last time, for both our sakes.

*

May I wake to the signs all around me and not be afraid to follow them. May the search for Truth always be my path through life.

*

Light up the way, dear Lord, for all Your children, especially those who struggle in the darkness, and suffer so much.

*

You are so vast and mysterious and that You should love me is almost beyond belief. We are all Your children and each one of us does our best. Please bless the little ones as they grow and learn. The world is going through a difficult time it seems, and there is a lot of upheaval for everyone, so many are experiencing great suffering. May Peace and Light be given to this beautiful planet and may Mankind, one day, all find Truth.

*

Just thinking: there are some people in my environment who will always see me as a "patient". People like me have to fight against the stigma of "Madness" and perhaps only in our hearts do we move beyond it. We walk alone, so is it surprising that our God walks with us.

*

For so many years, while I was ill, I was unable to do anything to help my sons and daughters and their families. Now, when perhaps it's too late, I am trying to be there for them, if I am needed. Bless them. They have learnt to walk their Path. Pete and I can just give a little support when it is needed.

*

My children all helped me through this illness, and when I was in hospital my daughter, Sue, brought me things, gave me a bath and cut my toenails. The others also visited me as often as they could, but most of all they brought their love, even though it was painful for them.

*

Dear Lord, not sleeping much but things are getting a bit clearer. Of course, as usual, I'm expecting changes overnight. There is lots of time if we are talking lifetimes! I now feel happy to let Peter tread his own Path to You; I know you will give him what he chooses for his journey. I love him and always will, in spite of the difficulties we have had, due in part because I haven't, up till now, been able to love myself.

*

I shall keep on trying to reach the inner part of myself. Self sometimes feels like just a tiny spark within. You know that my journey through life has not been an easy one, and You know that I am still concerned the mental illness might return. It's lasted thirty years, so I expect it's quite normal to sometimes feel this, especially if I have had a bad day, as everyone does.

*

Dear Lord, I said in my poetry that I was a schizophrenic and would not be afraid of the label. Now I feel like a rose beginning to bloom. Love seems to be the answer, never mind the labels. If I come from Love, then all will come out as it should.

*

Dear Lord, I think I know what I have done; I'm back to thinking I am not good enough even to approach You, and yet You say, over and over, that I am. I wonder if that doesn't include me, as I am mentally ill. I never used to think like this before I was mentally ill; must it haunt me all my days? I believe that Your love is with me, and that You understand these thoughts, which I so much want to change.

*

Dear Lord, just wanted to talk to You a little as I am thinking, now that I am walking better again, how can I be of use to the world around me? I want to shine my light, to show my love for You and my love for myself. It is not enough for me to drift through the days, cooking meals, doing jobs in the house, listening to music, reading, watching films and shopping for food.

*

May we all one day reach the Light within; Your presence is always near, and I don't feel I will ever be alone again. May Your Divine Love reach out to every soul on this planet and heal the suffering of all. If we are loved by You, then we need nothing more, for that is the greatest gift we can have.

*

I am more conscious now of the masses of people who are suffering in this world, with no awareness of You and no Light to ease the many trials they have to face. Having almost recovered from a serious mental illness, I would also like to help other sufferers to realise they do not have to stay in this nightmare. I would like to create something that might help.

*

I needed a laptop to write my story on, but I couldn't afford one. I spoke to my son, Steve. He said he would find me a laptop, and send it to me, which he did.

*

January 2008, my mum died, aged 90. February 4th, Mum's funeral. Such a day of joy and tears. Cried so much at the service and burial. God bless you, my dearest Mum. May your journey never cease till you reach the Lord of all Creation. It's very hard when you lose your mum, even though she is not far away. Bless you Mum, I will always love you.

*

It is all so simple, the light within guiding us on our way, as we face whatever may happen, work through it, then let it go, in the wonderful dance of life; the soul searching for itself.

*

We are on our way home. All the struggles are over and this world diminishes in our sight. Only the longing remains.

*

It was so good when families stayed together, but perhaps that's not the way it should be. They would certainly find Pete and I a handful! We keep funny hours, Pete drinks too much, I smoke too much, he likes T.V., I don't. I play my kind of music and he plays his, so how could they cope with us?

*

When I think of all I have written about life and my experiences... and yet what I haven't said is so wonderful; I just couldn't put it into words, no matter how I tried. I wonder if everyone is like this, each of us with a secret heart and soul that only God knows.

*

In 2012 I had a dream of my father crying and asking for forgiveness. I cried in the dream and woke up crying; a very healing dream.

*

I remember in my thirties struggling to find myself, so much to learn and constantly making mistakes. As one becomes older, it seems so incredibly simple, just a question of Love, and so good when the anger and fear are gone.

LONGING 1

How can I reach You, O Lord of my life?
In silence You speak to my heart
And I cannot hear what You say to me.
Are we closer yet, or still so far apart?

The way, at the moment, seems heavy.
Stones seem to cover my path.
All I have learnt seems as nothing.
I have forgotten how to laugh.

You show me a rose in a garden
Then show me a leaf on a tree.
Both of them truths in a lesson
That I am too lost to see.

That You love me, I can never doubt
As I stand in silence, at Your door,
Unworthy still, to enter in
And sleep and dream upon Your floor.

There are Masters here, upon this Earth
Who carry out Your Universal Plan.
They guide us with their wisdom,
If we listen, as best we can.

Joan.

LONGING 2

Another day, another time and I'm still here,
Waiting until You speak to me.
So many tears, a heart that bleeds
So lost until I reach Your door.

How can I speak to anyone
Of the love I feel inside?
You hold my heart, within Your hand
And never let me fall.

I may not find the answer
In this life or the next
But my heart says journey on
And love will do the rest.

We are only a drop in the ocean,
Only a grain in the sand,
Yet we all need Your love to discover
The light of Your beautiful land.

Please show me the steps that are needed,
Please show me the path I must tread,
A prisoner am I to Your wishes,
May You hear what I have said.

Joan.

10 THE ROAD TO RECOVERY

I am now in what the Mental Health Team call the Recovery Team. It is six years since my last relapse, and I am hoping I will never have another.

My injections of Redeptin, which I have been having for thirty years, have now been reduced from 10mg per fortnight to 3mg per fortnight. So life is looking much brighter and more positive.

When I came home after the last relapse in 2009, I was suffering from an allergic reaction to Depacote, which I had been given during the six months I was in hospital. It was stopped when I came home, but my hands were shaky and I could hardly walk at all. If I did try and walk it was like walking on sponge, and I couldn't feel the ground under my feet. My Doctor sent me to see a specialist, as he thought I might have Parkinson's disease. However the specialist tested me for Parkinson's and said I didn't have that; it was an allergic reaction to Depacote and would take about three years for the drug to get out of my system.

Over the last few years my legs have become a lot better, and although I still need a stick when I am outside, there is a big improvement. This has happened mostly through working hard on me, with books I have read like, "Your Body is telling you to Love Yourself", by Lise Bourbeau. I can highly recommend this book to anyone, as it covers over 500 illnesses and diseases.

My doctor is very pleased with how I am recovering and quite happy to let me explore alternative treatments, if it keeps me from prescription drugs, most of which I am allergic to.

Before I had my last relapse and was well, I travelled to Plymouth, where my parents lived then. I took care of them for a month, and came home for a month. I did this for two years.

The first journey I made to Plymouth, by train, was quite eventful. I met a strange little man who came and sat beside me and told me he was a warlock. I told him I was going to visit my parents, as my dad was very ill. He looked at me and said, "Your father wants you back." How could he have known of the problems I had suffered because of my dad, for most of my life? Out of this meeting came the poem I have written below, which I gave to my dad.

Father

Memories of childhood days
Haunt this wintry morning.
Songs you sang to me of
Pretty Redwing, and Two Little Girls in Blue.

Then I grew afraid of you,
The stern voice and the martial air
And the stranger I met on a train
Said, "Your father wants you back."

So I came back to you
And loved you, not for your faults
But in spite of them,
Learnt forgiveness and compassion
For all the pain you endured.

When madness threatened to overwhelm me
You were there, sat before the High Judge,
So I pleaded your case and fought
For your redemption, and my own.
And God forgave us both.

Now your eyes grow dim
And a new life beckons you.
Love has lit the lamps, to light your way.
So take heart and journey on,
Knowing that I love you.

Joan.

When my dad died at 88 years old, my mother said "We never had a cross word." I smiled at this, as they were still having arguments when I visited them. I helped my dad get dressed and used a heat lamp on his painful joints. Sometimes we would play cards in the evening, if he was awake and well enough. He was still capable of getting angry if he was losing at cards, but somehow I had lost my fear of him, which was great. I also wrote a poem to my mum, just to let her know how much I loved her.

Mother

Mother, my dearest friend,
Lover of gentle things, with a heart
As large as the sun;
Join me in a celebration of life.

You gave me room to breathe and dream
And your song has been a song of love.
I know that you get fearful of the future
But if you could only look inside,
You would find the answer.

And we, your daughters, all follow you.
We will not be far behind
So let our love surround you.
The journey has no end.

You gave me life, a tiny frail thing
And your voice has been a blessing
And your laughter has brightened
Many of my difficult hours.

We must all tread our Path,
Find within the strength we need.
I greet you as a fellow traveller.
The Dance goes on forever.

Joan.

So on my road to recovery, I have made my peace with my dad at last.

Sometimes I feel so sad for Peter, the T.I.A.'s and heart problems he has had have affected him so much. He sometimes seems so unhappy, and I feel helpless to do anything to ease it. He was retired through illness, from his travelling and work, selling books. Now at 82, he seems to have lost some of the joy of living, and puts all his efforts into looking after our 8 cats (all strays), helping me with the housework and shopping. He loves gardening in the summer and watching T.V. I think he may resent the time he has spent taking care of me through my illness, which has prevented him treading his own Path. I try and tell him how much better I am now, but I don't know if he believes that.

He grieved so much when I became schizophrenic and he thought I would never come home from hospital. I will always be grateful to him for all the love and care he gave me when I needed it, but he doesn't have to do that anymore. Poor darling, he is worn out with it all and needs some joy back in his life. May he feel happier, as I grow stronger.

Keeping love alive when I am 73 and Pete is 82 needs to be constantly worked at. There can be no love without compassion and understanding. Some things are harder, but giving each other the freedom to be, and love yourself, is easier without the passion and demands of youth. We grow old gracefully.

One of the greatest things I have learnt from life is first to forgive yourself and then to forgive those around you. God's greatest gift to us all is Forgiveness and Love. None of us are perfect, and we all make mistakes, but the important thing is to let go and be kind to yourself.

People with schizophrenia, or any form of mental illness, are no different from everybody else. We may appear a little strange at times, especially when we seem to live in a different world, but please don't shun us or label us with stigmas that only apply to a few. I realise people must be kept safe, but there is far more anger and violence in the normal world than there ever is in the mentally ill person's world.

To lock us away, dose us full of drugs, is only an answer to a few individuals. There must be one to one communication, so that we can say the Truth as we see it. Some of us have a greater understanding of the path of life than we are given credit for. So please don't be afraid of us. Most of the time, we tread the road to recovery alone and rejected by the world. May this attitude change, one day soon?

11 HEALING GUIDANCE FOR THE FUTURE

Blessing

Life can be a blessing
To each and everyone
With joy and tears around us
And adventures, full of fun.

I hold a rose, its beauty see
A message in each petal ,
Forget the past, find Truth at last
Dancing into Eternity.

Tread softly stranger, where you walk
Your feet on sacred ground,
This Earth is ours for a moment;
Protect it and make no sound.

I believe that the people who suffer from schizophrenia may have had very different experiences compared with mine. I also feel they should not be labelled as mentally ill, but seen for the unique people they are.

I think our stories need to be listened to, in order for others to see the truth as we see it. One day, the medical profession may realise that these stories often contain seeds of wisdom. There should also be a change of consciousness in understanding the many dimensions of our minds and souls.

I do not deny the fact that a minority of people with schizophrenia do sometimes commit acts of violence and harm, but this is also common in everyday life by normal people. Those of us who are labelled schizophrenic have to bear the stigma, and are not treated as individuals; most of the people with schizophrenia are very gentle and kind and wouldn't hurt anyone.

I suppose I must be considered one of the lucky ones, as I am in recovery from this illness. However, I am not sorry for the experiences I have had, comprising great pain but also great joy.

At times it is difficult to live in the normal world with all its distractions, and the speed it moves around at. Of course I am happy for my family, who worry less when I am well. I think though, for my own peace of mind, I will still continue to be an eccentric woman.

I have compiled some healing guidelines that have helped me, and I hope that they may help you, if you feel you need them.

1. Meditation calms the body and heals the mind.
2. I think our role in life is to help people appreciate their lives.
3. The health of our inner life plays an important role in healing.
4. Always keep near you books, phone numbers, music and films that can lift your life into a better place.
5. Live every day as precious, and every positive thought as a light in the darkness.
6. Instead of being full of fear, replace it with the search for Truth, and you will come across a place of healing.
7. The power of love and compassion can overcome all the negative feelings that destroy us.
8. Noticing signs that are dangerous, that we need to do something about, can be a healing tool.

9.   Always believe in the right to be who, and what, you are.
10. It is never too late to overcome the past.
11. By understanding and exploring the effects of my illness, I am now able to know the signs, to prevent another relapse, because I am stronger.

I have now reached the present moment, and my story has been written. Nobody can tell what the future holds for any of us, but I have no fear of dying. That is a door opening, not a door closing. I am simply moving along on this wonderful journey through Life and beyond.

Thank you for being with me for a while. May Love and Light be in your life always.

Suggested Reading

Conversations with God, Books 1, 2, and 3, By Neale Donald Walsch.

The Dreamseller, by Augusto Cury.

The Prophet, by Kahlil Gibran.

Your Body's Telling You Love Yourself, by Lise Bourbeau.

Jonathan Livingston Seagull, by Richard Bach

Printed in Great Britain
by Amazon